# Cheaper Than Therapy

## How to Keep Life's Small Problems
## from Becoming Big Ones

*For Phil —*
*a Neighbor (LES)*
*in Spirit!*

*The Lesson*
*of the Paper Clips*

*Gina Greenlee*

Photo-illustrations by
David Schulz

Aventine Press
1023 4th Avenue, Suite 204
San Diego, CA 92101

ISBN: 1-59330-292-4
Printed in the United States of America

For Abbe and Robin
Teachers, Mothers, Therapists

# Introduction

*Paper clips can help me have fewer problems in life?* *You've got to be kidding.*

No, I'm not. In this book, paper clips are a symbol for behavior.

*Why paper clips?* Because they're everywhere – the office, school, library, copy center, and at home. If we examine how we interact with paper clips, we can alter our lives.

I once had a part-time job where all I did for 20 hours a week was paper clip printouts of computer screens. By the end of a two-year stint, I had gone through cartons of clips.

I never bothered plucking the paper clips from their tiny boxes. I preferred a more preschool approach and dumped them on my desk to form a shiny paper clip volcano.

On occasion, I'd reach for a clip that had hitched a ride with one, two, sometimes three other clips and, in frustration, fling the clingy bunch across my desk. After a week, a new pile formed, entirely of bunched paper clips. I'd created for myself a second, even less exciting job.

Without pay.

This happened repeatedly. Then one day I learned my lesson: Two or three tangled clips were a signal to stop what I was doing and deal with the pesky pieces of wire rather than letting them accumulate for a week. I didn't like having to disrupt my daily workflow to occasionally untangle clips, but I liked having to unknot a week's worth a whole lot less.

The day I learned my paper clips lesson – small problems become big problems when I ignore them – was the day I realized I behaved this way in other areas of my life, whether it was procrastination in bringing my writing ideas to the marketplace, managing debt, or hanging on to relationships that had stopped working long ago. The choices I made when interacting with paper clips were a metaphor for how I lived.

Is it just me? How do other people react to this same fork in the road? Do they say "the heck with it" and toss the tangled paper clips aside to reach for the single one? Or, do they make a choice that's a little uncomfortable at first but pays off down the road? What other options exist? Suppose people viewed their interactions with paper clips as a metaphor? How would that affect them?

These questions form the heart of *Cheaper Than Therapy: How to Keep Life's Small Problems from Becoming Big Ones*, presented for you to explore and answer for your own life.

*The Lesson of the Paper Clips* is an opportunity to observe and learn from personal problem-solving patterns and, should we choose, transform how we live.

It's also cheaper than therapy.

Gina Greenlee
Hartford, Connecticut
May 2005

The paper clip.

Curved wire.

Nothing more.

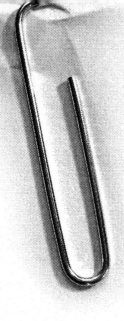

Still, a gem of an
invention.

# At times,
## a distraction…

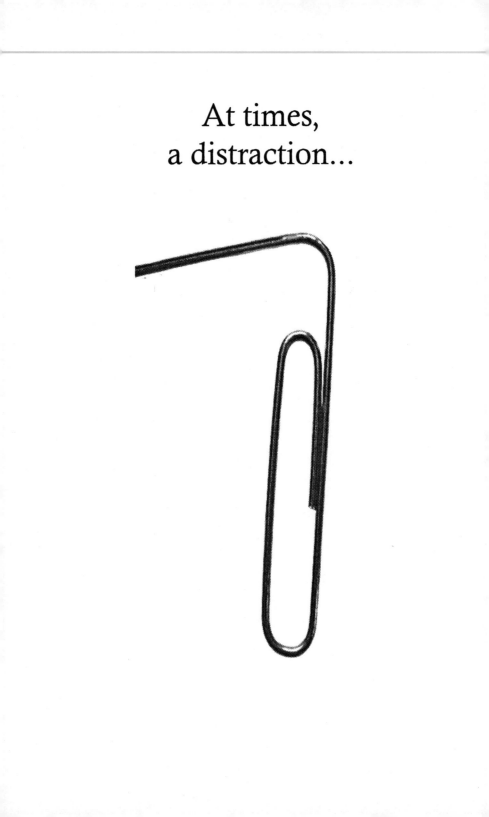

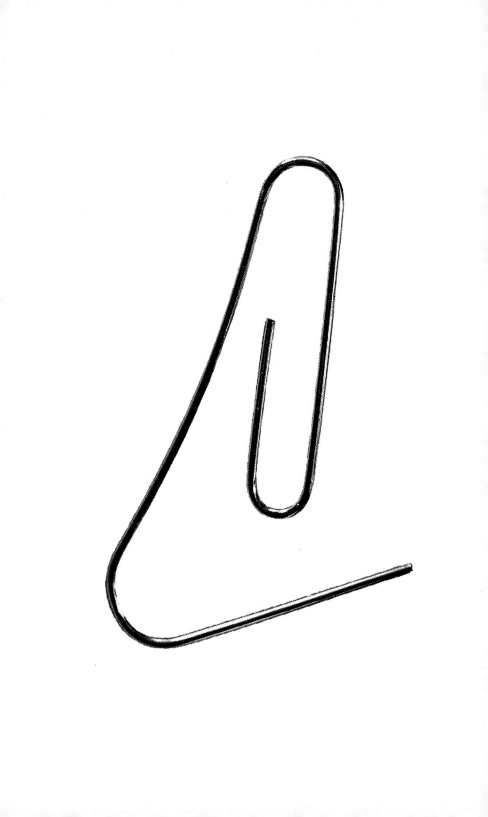

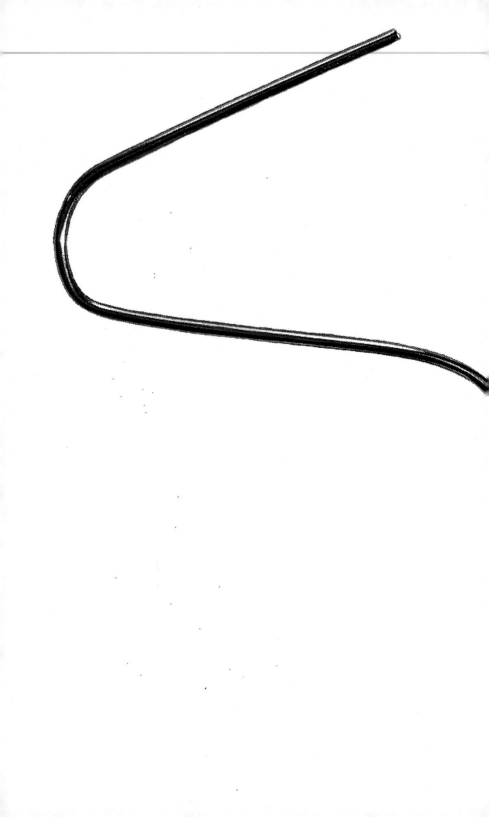

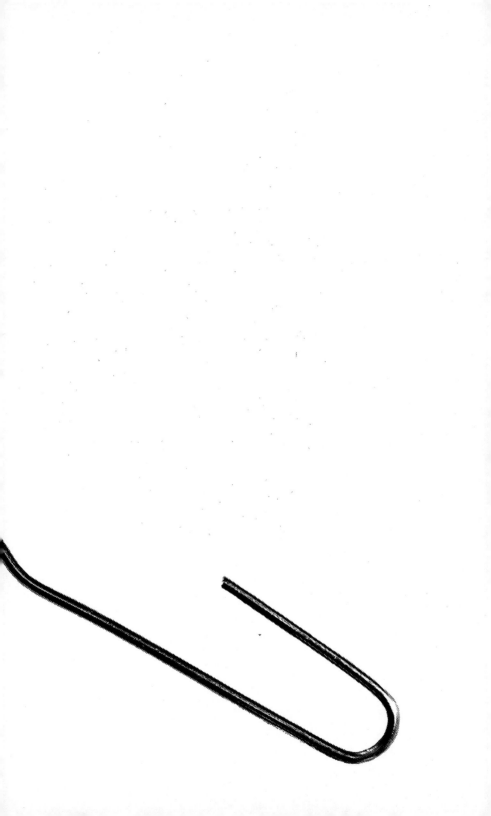

...yet ready

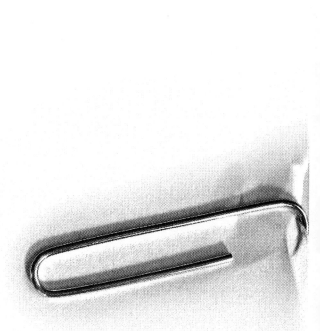

to work again...

...and again.

Until

a will to merge
emerges.

And

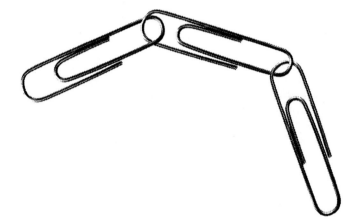

multiplies.

Do we tackle this
small problem?

# Or reach for an easy way out?

Easy outs work.

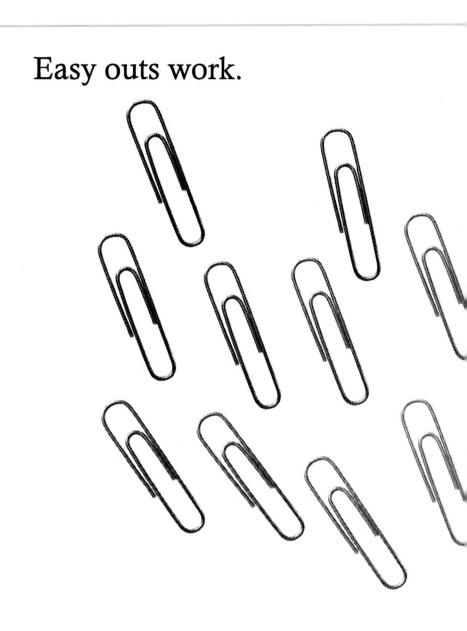

Until we exhaust them.

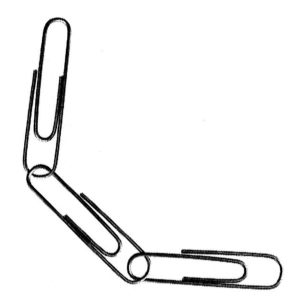

And wind up
with the small problem
we tried to avoid
from the start.

If we keep avoiding
small problems...

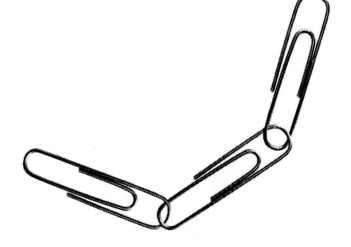

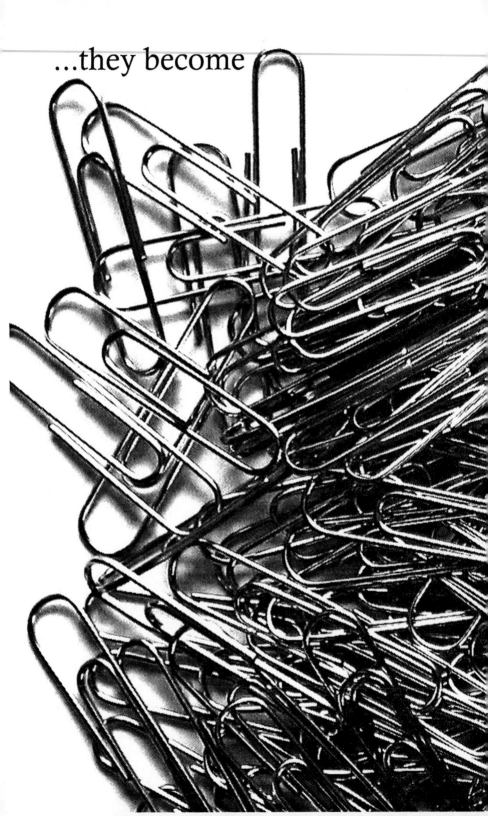

...they become

big ones.

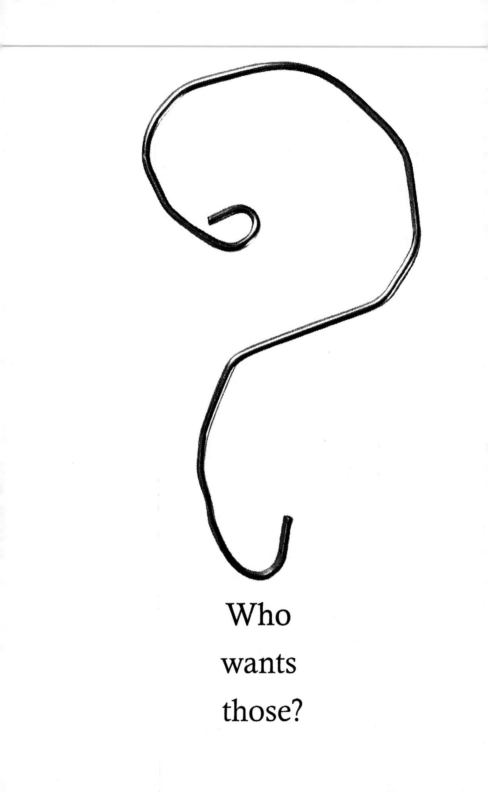

Who
wants
those?

The easy way out...

...is a trickster.

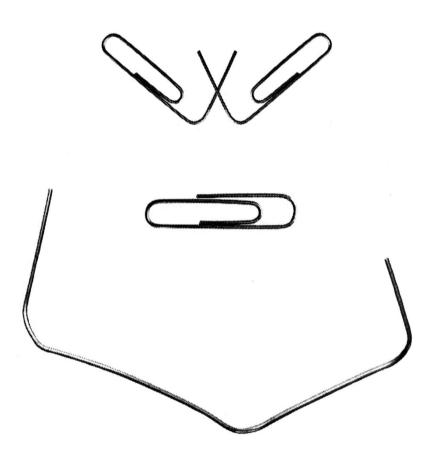

Because
it only delays
what we eventually
must face.

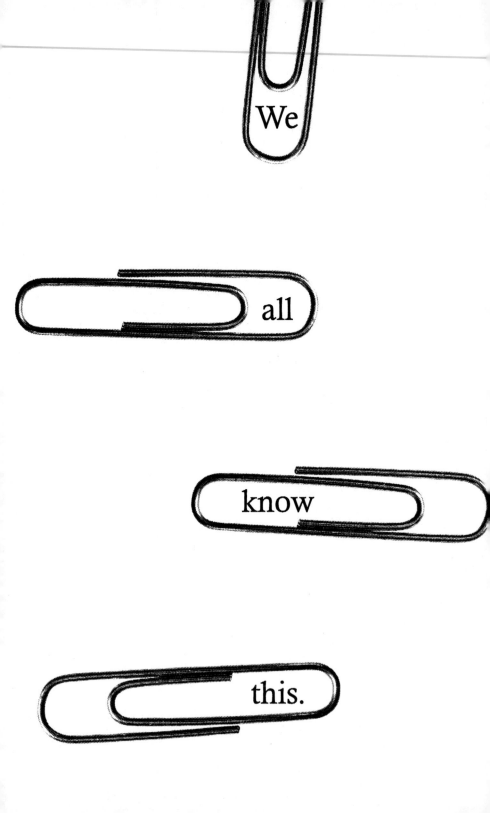

# So,

# why do we choose
# the easy way out?

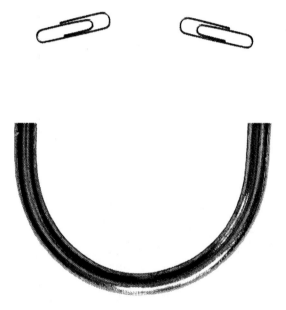

Because it's comfortable.

Because we can
avoid feeling
squirmy
and
bothered

like when
we wear
a tight belt or
a scratchy bra.

Because we'd rather do
what we are used to doing.

To act when
confronted
with small
problems

means

being willing
to be
uncomfortable.

Why would we
want to do
that
?

Because the more comfortable
we are with discomfort,
the more discomfort we can
tolerate.

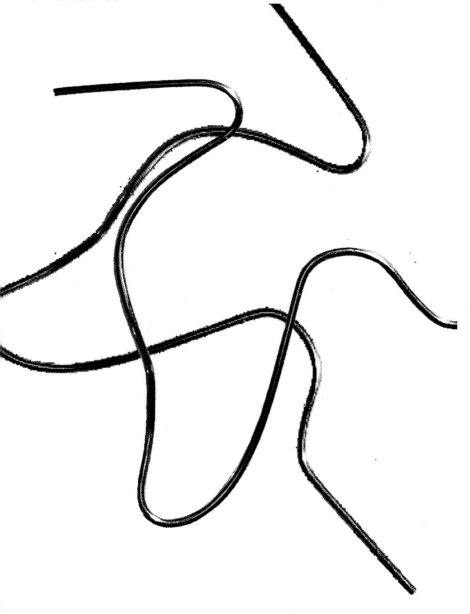

In other words,
every time we
handle a small
problem,

it gets easier
to take on
new ones.

That's how we expand
our "comfort zone"

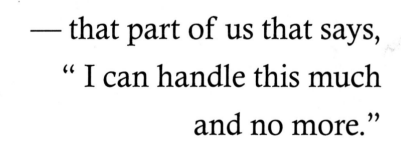

— that part of us that says,
" I can handle this much
and no more."

The trick is to expand
our comfort zone
a little at a time
so we don't become
overwhelmed.

Consistent action over time

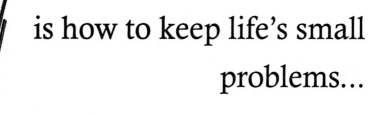

is how to keep life's small problems...

...from becoming big ones.

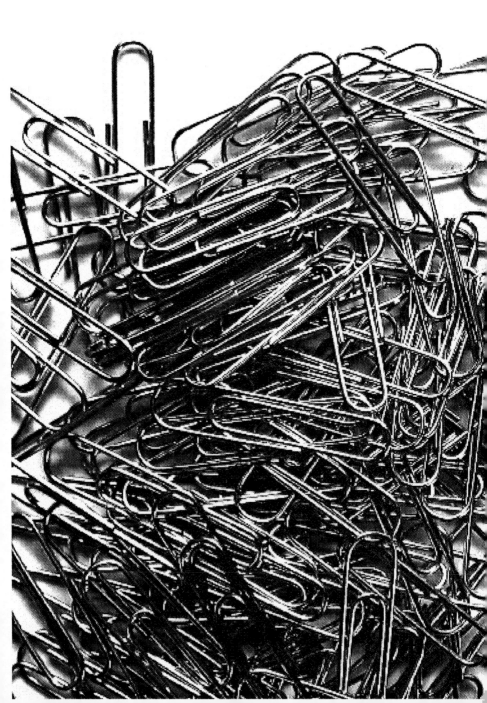

We can
practice this
when
we use
paper clips.

We
can?

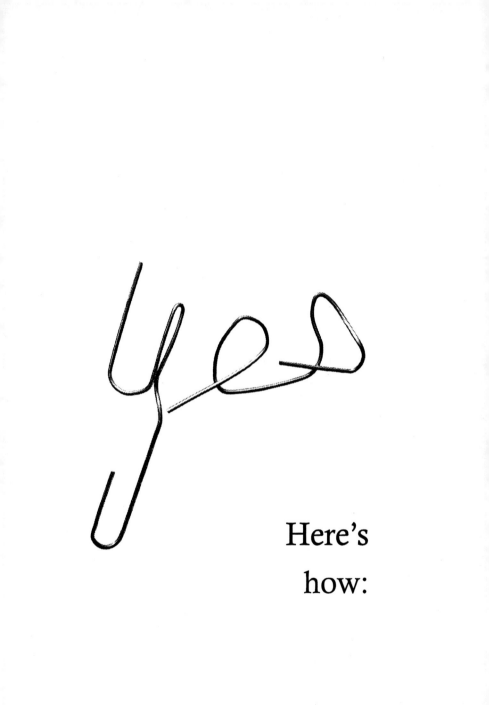

Here's
how:

The next time
you have a choice
between

reaching for

an easy way out

or handling
a small problem
as it occurs...

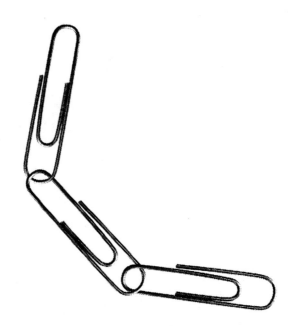

...choose to handle the small problem.

Each time you handle a
small problem as it occurs,

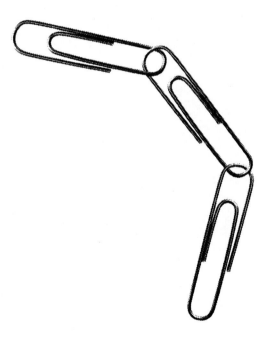

you accomplish three things:

# 1

You strengthen
your tolerance
for discomfort.

It's like exercise. The more you do it, the stronger you become while experiencing fewer aches and pains.

# 2

You expand your comfort zone.

As it expands,
you can handle more
with less discomfort
because problems
that used to be outside
your comfort zone

are now
inside.

# 3

You form a habit.

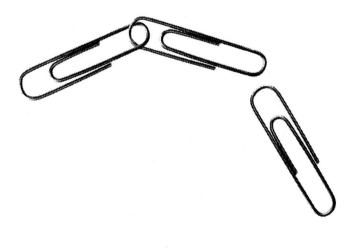

This takes
practice.
It's how
you establish
any skill.

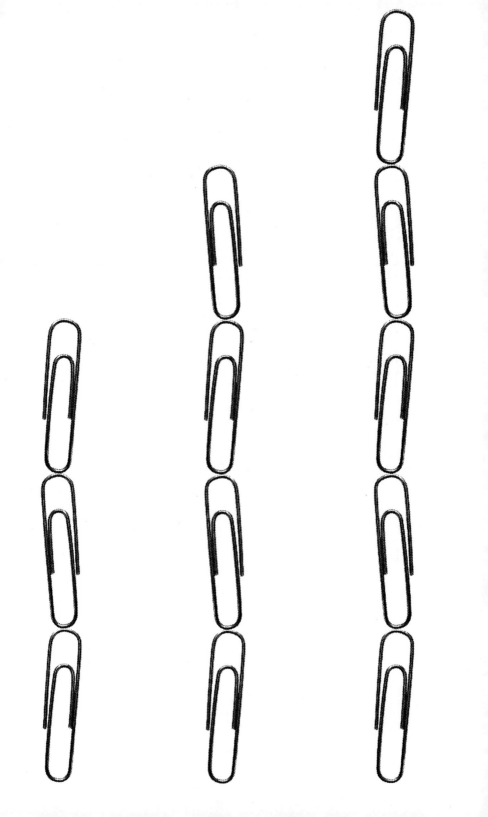

Over time,
handling small problems
becomes second nature,
like riding a bicycle
(or anything else that took
a while to learn but you
now do easily without
too much thought).

You'll notice a tendency,
in different areas of your life,
to confront what you used to
put off or ignore —

until it became overwhelming.

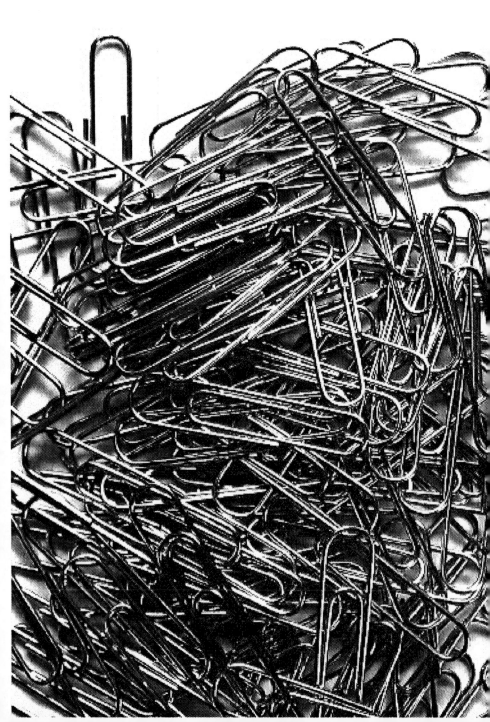

Whether you reach
for an easy way out

or

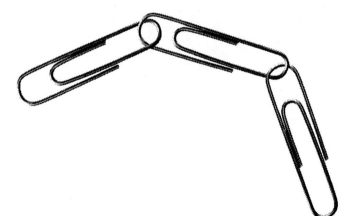

handle small problems
as they occur,

you are establishing a pattern
for how you live.

# This pattern
will show up in different areas
of your life:

Work.

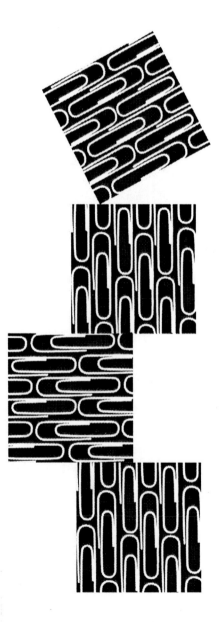

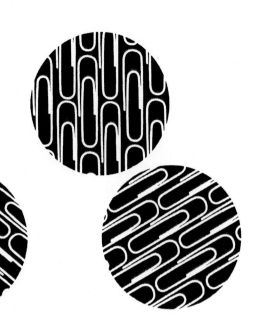

Money.

Relationships.

# This pattern
## isn't all one way

## or the other.

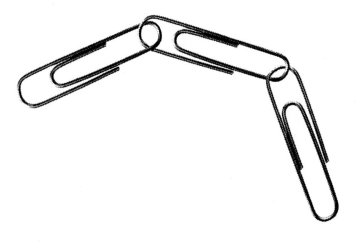

That means

in some areas of our lives,

we are doers.

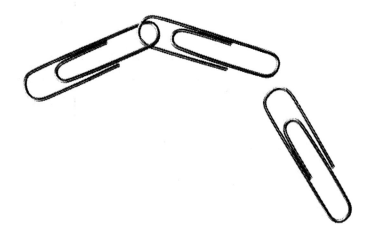

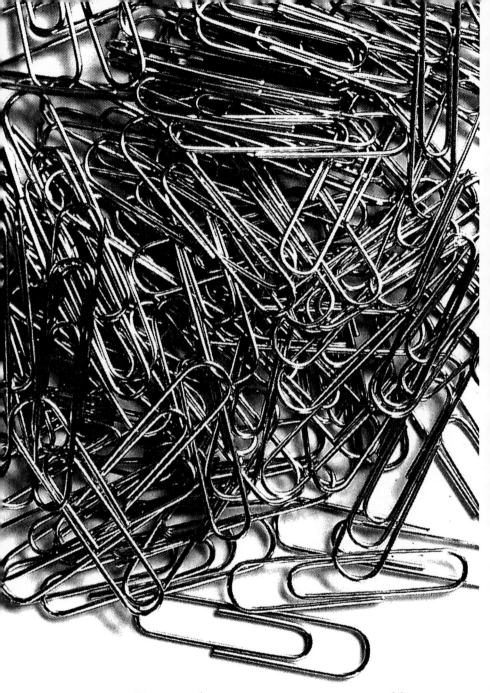

In other areas, we allow
situations to pile up before we act.

Our patterns are not ingrained; they can shift in response to our experiences.

Our response to life
events and changes in
our perspective
can cause
old piles to dwindle
with action,

and new piles to form
where once there were none.

Even if our preferred pattern is to always act,

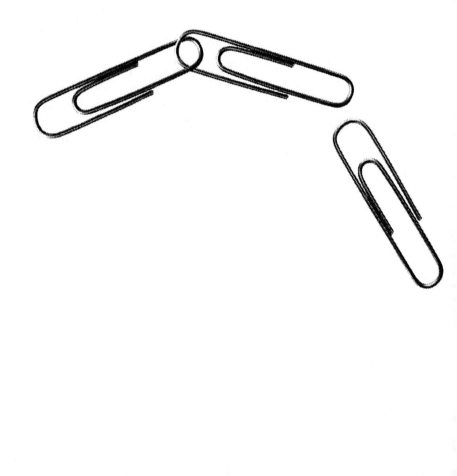

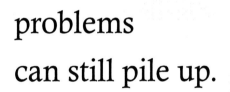

problems

can still pile up.

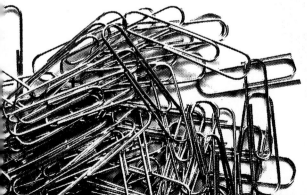

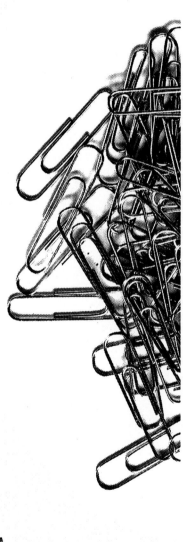

Even if our preferred
pattern is to seldom act,

eventually
we must if
we want to
function.

What we
can keep
constant
is our
observation
of where our
problems are
piling up or
dwindling,
and how fast.

A fragment of curved wire
can create in us the habit of
awareness.

It reminds us that we
can shift our attention to
where it is needed most at
any given time —

whether to prevent problems, keep small ones from becoming big ones, or cause big ones to disappear.

That's the lesson
of the paper clips.

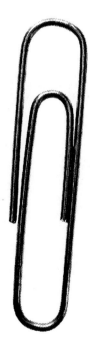

And, it's cheaper than therapy.

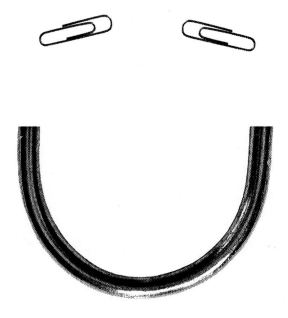

# A Note about Therapy

This book's title is factual: *The Lesson of the Paper Clips* is cheaper than therapy. For the past decade, I've used therapy as a tool for personal growth. During that time, my therapists have shared many wonderful books with me; some of them have profoundly affected my life.

I hope this book appeals to a wide range of readers in and out of therapy, as well as those who never intend to visit a therapist. Also, I hope therapists find this book to be one worth sharing with their clients as an adjunct to their work.

I'd love to hear from readers about how *The Lesson of the Papers Clips* has affected their lives.

Please contact me: gina@ginagreenlee.com.

*About the Author*

GINA GREENLEE is a freelance columnist for *The Hartford Courant*. She is a frequent contributor to *Essence Magazine* and has written for the *St. Petersburg Times*. Her *New York Times Magazine* personal essay, *No Tears for Frankie*, has been reprinted in the essay collections *Four in One* (Longman Publishers, 2004) and *Paragraphs and Essays* (Houghton-Mifflin, 2005). This is her first book.

*About the Illustrator*

DAVID SCHULZ is a freelance graphic designer, illustrator, painter and set designer. He has illustrated a number of children's books. This is his first book for adults. He lives with his wife and a couple of old pets in Connecticut.

# With Appreciation and Gratitude

Sharon Anderson

Author's Guild

Beth Bruno

Deb Caswell

Tracie Clayton-Hom

Connecticut Authors and Publishers Association

Jeanne Dursi

Beth Gibbs

Margaret Greenberg

Neal Greenberg

Beth Lipton

Peter Loffredo

Carolyn Lumsden

Carla D. Marshall Greenleaf

Ron Masse

Steve McDermott

National Writers Union

Liz Petry

Scott Raymond

Sylvia Ruckens

David Schulz

Michael Staufacker

Dan Uitti

# COMING JUNE 2006

Cheaper Than Therapy

How to Take the Risks You Need
to Create the Life You Want

*The Lesson of the Chopsticks*

Visit www.ginagreenlee.com

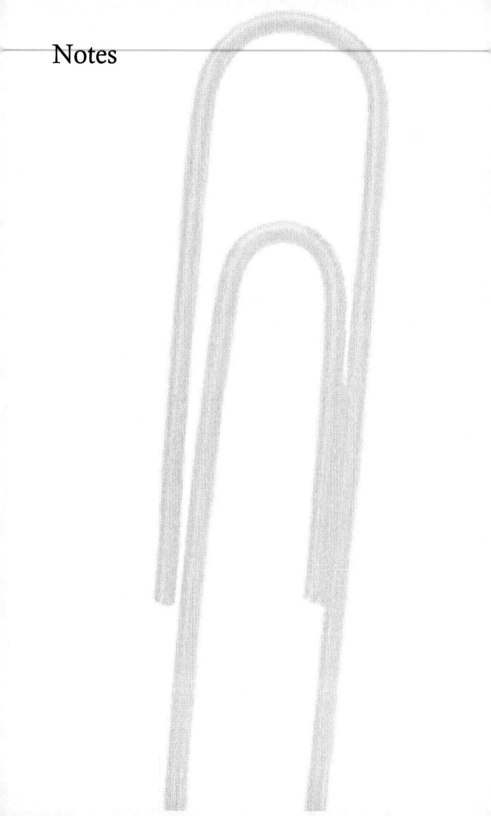

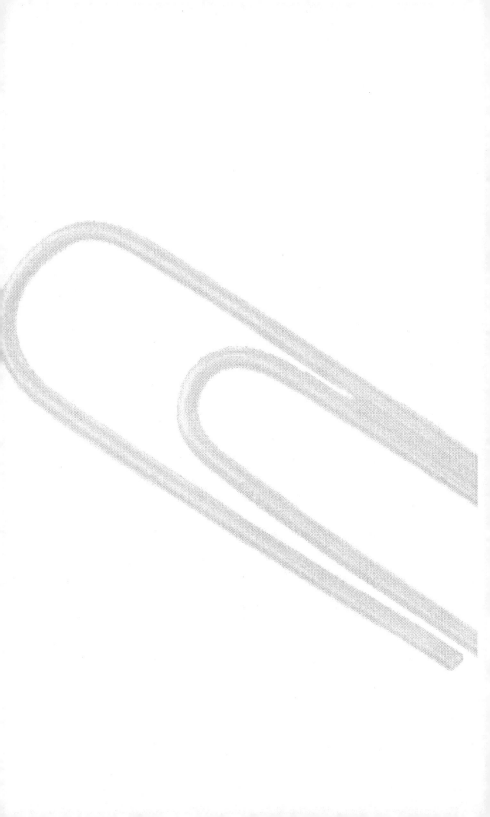

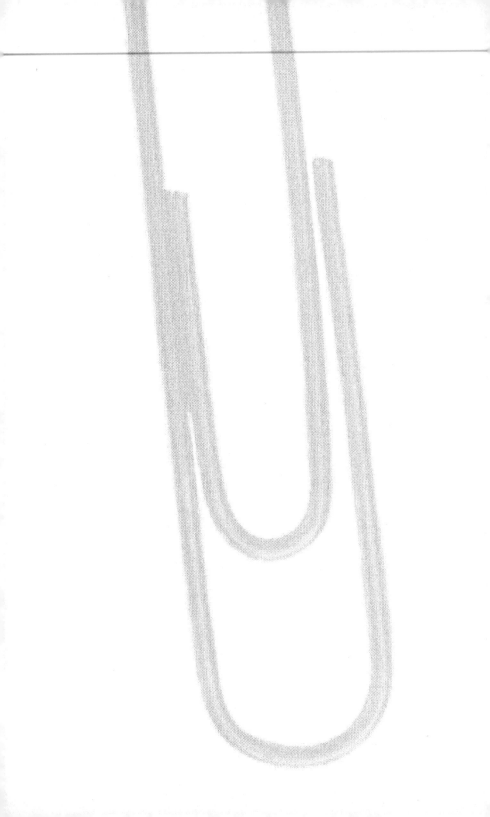

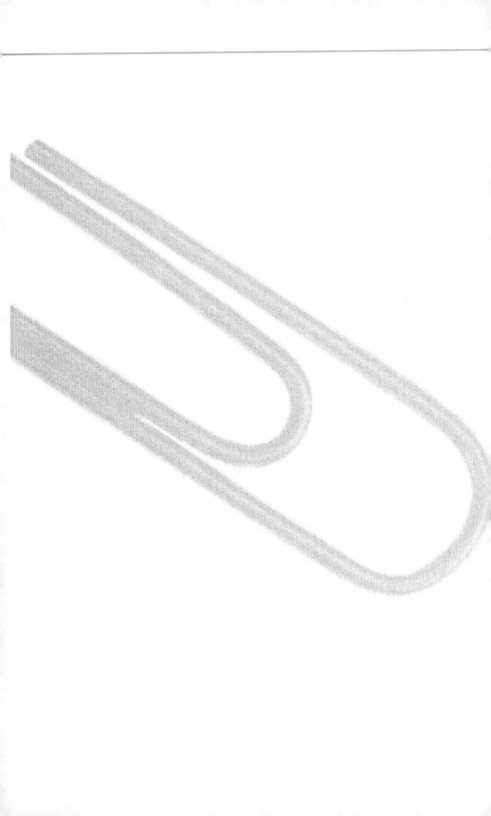

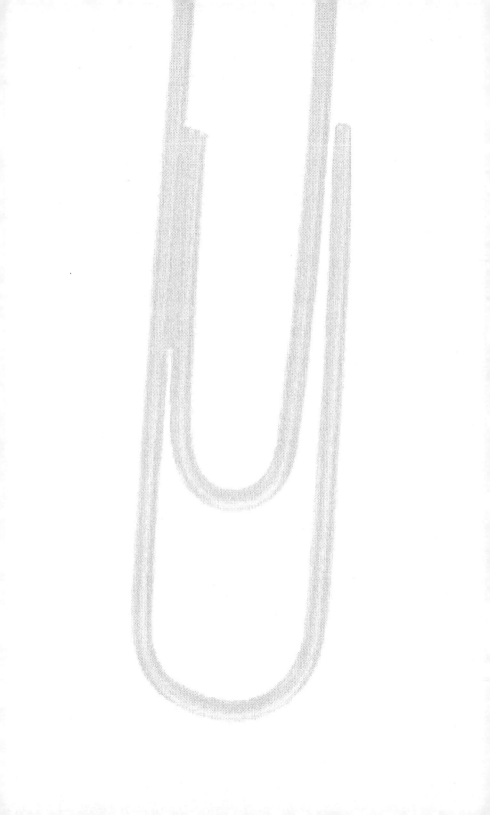

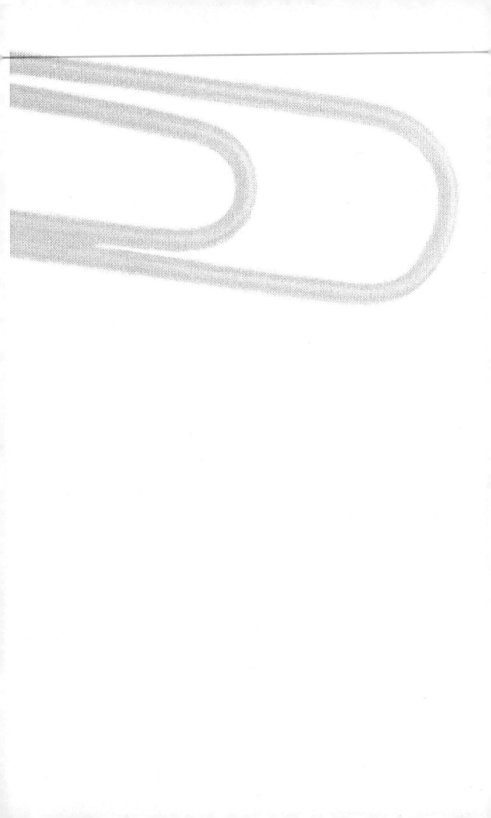

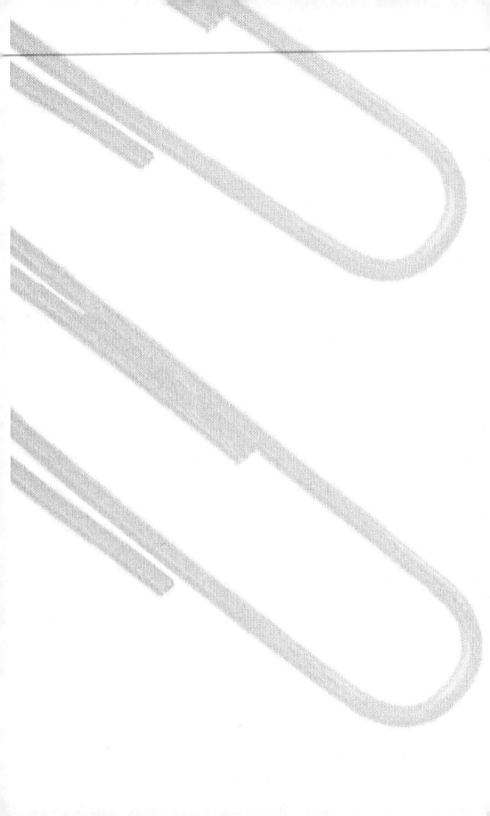

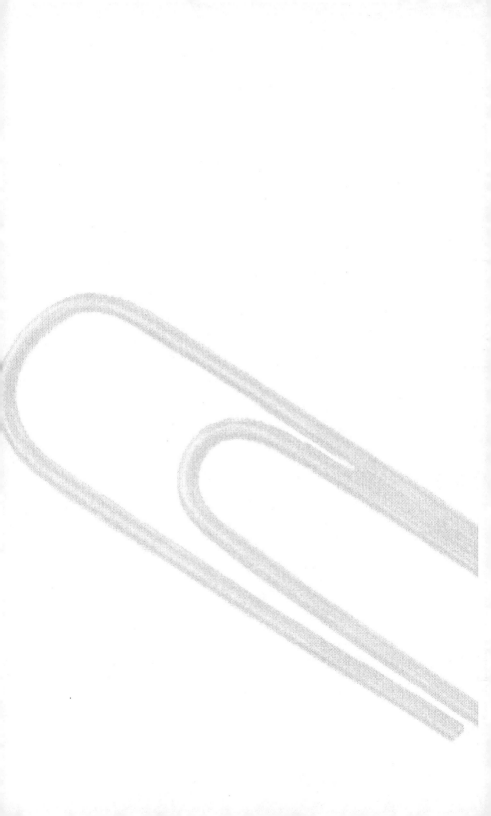

*Paper clips can help me have fewer problems in life? You've got to b* kidding.

Let the lesson begin…

Printed in the United States
36907LVS00001B/1-204

9 781593 302924